POWERFUL KEYS to SPIRITUAL SIGHT

MICHAEL VAN VLYMEN

INTRODUCTION

Spiritual sight has become a very hot topic in these present times. Whether we call it spiritual sight, discerning of spirits or seeing in the spiritual realm, there are a lot of people today who want to know if this can become their reality. We have heard the testimonies of the visitations from the Lord, angels and more and want this for ourselves. That's good because the Lord wants us to have it. The Bible clearly states that we should "Fix our eyes on those things that are unseen…" (2 Corinthians 4:18)

This Pocket-Book "Powerful Keys to Spiritual Sight" was created to give those of you seeking spiritual sight a Biblical overview to follow so that this can become your reality too. This book will present material very similar to my previous book "How to See in the Spirit." This Pocket Book version was created so that a smaller, focused and helpful book of instructions would exist that could easily be carried and translated into different languages and transportable across the world. . In this book I explain the concepts of spiritual sight much like I would if I had only twenty minutes to explain to you how to learn to see in the spirit. I try to present what I consider the most important things that I would want you to understand so that your eyes can be opened the way the Lord intended.

MICHAEL VAN VLYMEN

CONTENTS

PREFACE

As I laid down to go to sleep, I prayed "Lord please let your angels minister to me in some way." My head had only been on the pillow for a few minutes and I had not yet closed my eyes when something spectacular happened. Suddenly an angel materialized only eight to ten feet away from me and began walking toward me. He was about six feet tall with dark hair and eyes and he was dressed as a warrior or knight would dress. The expression on his face was serious but his eyes said he was also kind. As he approached me he extended his hand over me and when he got close enough he laid his hand on me. When he touched me I went out like a light….

This "story" is far from over. When your spiritual eyes are open, these kinds of events will become your normal life. An ongoing and ever unfolding relationship with God that is an adventure and a journey of discovery beyond anything that you could hope or dream. It is my sincere desire and prayer that you pursue Jesus Christ and this Biblical reality with all of your heart. There is literally nothing that this world has to offer that even comes close to the things of the Kingdom of God. So if you are a follower of Christ, follow with all your heart. If you are not, ask Jesus to forgive all your sins and turn your heart to Him and ask Him to be your Savior and Lord. Now……Let's begin this journey together.

MICHAEL VAN VLYMEN

1

THE REALITY OF THE UNSEEN REALM

There are two realms that we live in. One realm is the seen realm or natural realm and the other is the spiritual realm. Many of us have no or very little awareness of the spiritual realm even though we continually engage that realm every day. Let's become aware.

Our lives can take on greater meaning when we open our spiritual eyes. Whatever your relationship with God is now, if your spiritual eyes are opened that relationship goes into the stratosphere, far beyond anything you could ever imagine. The Bible actually tells us to look on the unseen so we have confidence that this reality is for us.

So we fix our eyes not on what is seen, but on what is unseen, since what is seen is temporary, but what is unseen is eternal. (2 Corinthians 4:18)

God created us with spiritual eyes and He did that so that we could see in the spirit. The world of Heaven, the saints, angels, evil spirits, and even the Lord himself is right in front of us in another dimension...a spiritual dimension. We can remove the things that hinder us from seeing and learn to see in the spiritual realm and interact with Heaven. That's what this book is about.

What can you do to make the unseen realm seen? That is the question many people are asking nowadays. People in the church world are talking about visitations from angels and the Lord, others are talking about trips to Heaven, seeing the Sea of Glass, the Throne, the Hall of Faith and other places. People outside of the church community are also seeking deeper spiritual things, knowing there is something more but not sure exactly what.

I will tell you right up-front. I have had some experience in this reality and if you pursue anything of a spiritual nature, it should be Jesus Christ and His Kingdom. Give yourself to Him and let Him reveal these spiritual truths to you. Let Him surround you with angels and protect you and give you His peace and joy. It doesn't matter how great your gift is to see in the spirit if you are living in fear or unrest. Jesus gives us a spiritual inheritance plus the love, joy and peace and eternal security. I unashamedly tell you that Jesus is God. He can and will prove it to you. Making up our own "reality" of what spiritual truth is because it's something that sounds good to us is *not* truth, it's self- deception. So pursue Jesus and pursue spiritual sight through His provisions.

What Blocks our Sight?

When we are born our spiritual eyes are seeing just fine for the most part. If you have ever watched babies or small children very much, you can see them looking at seemingly empty space, sometimes even smiling or reaching out. When children get a little older, toddler age for example many of them have invisible friends that they play with or talk to. Many parents come into a room to see their daughter having a tea party complete with real conversations with a "pretend" guest or a son playing with toys showing things to an "imaginary" playmate.

If we could bring ourselves to leave that alone, our kids would grow up seeing the unseen realm and keeping the ability to do so but because we normally don't have a grid for this we talk them out of the ability to see the spiritual realm. "Janet there is no one there. Your friend is pretend." "Johnny your friend isn't real he is just in your imagination." It only takes a couple years of them hearing how displeased their parents are that they acknowledge this friend that they stop. They turn off the ability to see through a desire to please the parents or the authority figure in their life whoever it is.

That is the beginning of the end of spiritual sight. As we grow up we see many things that harm our spiritual eyes or damage them. Unclean images, scary images, traumatic things that further cut off our spiritual sight. If we grow up in certain religious orders we are taught that spiritual things or the spiritual realm is demonic and dangerous and that creates even more obstructions for us.

Further Obstructions

To complicate matters even more, there are actual spiritual veils and scales that can cover our eyes to make it hard or even impossible to see in the spirit. These veils are created by sins, fears, traumas, doubt, unbelief, emotional damage of different sorts, distractions, physical ailments and a host of other things. The great news is that all of these things can be dealt with so that our sight can be restored.

I have seen the veils and the scales and I have seen them fall to the ground like dust so that they no longer affected me as my own eyes were opened. When seeing the spirit realm, sometimes you can see these veils hanging like dark, sheer curtains and floating in front of you blocking your sight. Sometimes there are lots of them and it makes it even harder. But there is an answer.

Holy Purpose

If you have a desire for your spiritual eyes to be opened and your desire is for the plans and purposes of God, He will facilitate the opening of your eyes. Our relationship with Christ gives us a place of legal right to enter into this realm and reality. (John 10:2)

Preparations for the Spirit

As your eyes open to the spiritual realm it can be quite daunting even if you feel you are well prepared. Throughout the Bible we see angels telling people *"Don't be afraid."* It is something most of us are not used to.

The adjustment to this realm can be easily made by diving into the Word of God, The Bible. The entire Bible is full of spiritual beings, situations, manifestations and adventures. Get into the Word and study (2 Timothy 2:15) and get used to the spiritual reality. Set your mind and your affections on spiritual things. Think about spiritual things. See how our role models acted and reacted in these spiritual and supernatural encounters. Know the Word. Live by the Word. Act on the Word.

Another important reason for knowing the Word is that we have to know who we are in Christ and what our authority is especially concerning these spiritual things. The unseen realm is inhabited by evil spirits as well as angels and sometimes we have to deal with these beings. (Whether we see them or not) Knowing the Word gives us an assurance and peace that we can deal with evil spirits and fear has no power over us to block our sight.

I have given you authority to trample on snakes and scorpions and to overcome all the power of the enemy; nothing will harm you. (Luke 10:19)

Another Important Reality

The unseen realm has incredible power and sway over the seen realm. Illnesses, pains, emotions, fears, problems of every kind can either be created from the unseen realm or manipulated by that realm. If you see the unseen, it gives you an advantage.. Things can't trick you so easily. You can actually see the temptations as they really look in the spirit. You know what is *really* going on around you.

You can see a problem long before it becomes one and deal with things that others are not aware of.

There have been many times that I see something that I know is not from God coming into my home. Sometimes they are dark figures, unclean creatures of different sorts or even people. I can rebuke them in the authority of Jesus Christ and drive them out before they ever become a problem for my family. What are these things? Sometimes you will know, other times you won't. They can be anything from spirits of anger, fear, illness, bad dreams or a host of other things. If you engage the reality of the unseen, you can deal with all of this and protect your loved ones.

Can you pray and protect your home even if you don't see? Of course. We have authority whether we see or not. But God gave us eyes to see so let's take advantage of that benefit. The Lord Jesus paid a very high price to give us a wonderful inheritance including but not limited to our salvation. Let's receive everything that He provided.

This little book is not written to convince you that this is Biblical or that it is for you. Read the Word and see what it says and make up your own mind concerning this. We have the Word and that is what it's for, to judge things by. If you believe that God wants your eyes to see, then pursue this. If you believe God does not want them to see then don't pursue this. If you need a hint, God does not want His children to be spiritually blind. Believe me.

I pray you make the wise choice.

2
WAITING ON THE LORD

I am going to start with one of the most helpful and effective things that you can ever do to open your spiritual eyes or engage in any spiritual reality.

First I will explain what this is and what our Biblical right is to do this and then I will give the practical points and what the fruit of this practice can be. If you take nothing else from the book, please read this chapter carefully and do this.

An Explanation

Waiting on the Lord is when we take time to sit before him, with a desire to know him and be close to Him, expecting Him to reveal himself to us.
As we draw close to Him, He draws close to us. This is a time of stillness, quiet, focus on Him, desire and

expectation. There is Biblical precedent of course. The Psalms talk about how King David waited on the Lord a lot.

Lead me in thy truth, and teach me: for thou art the God of my salvation; on thee do I wait all the day. (Psalm 25:5)

And because we suggest that you wait on the Lord in stillness during these times, here is a scripture.

Be still, and know that I am God: I will be exalted among the heathen, I will be exalted in the earth. (Psalm 46:10)

How Does Waiting Open Your Eyes?

Waiting on the Lord is coming aside to forget about the physical world and it's problems and focus on the Lord and the Kingdom of Heaven. You are shifting your *focus.* You stop looking at the physical and start looking for the spiritual.

The Process

First of all we need to realize that as we pursue God or anything in the Kingdom of Heaven, we have to accept the help of the helper...the Holy Spirit. The Holy Spirit is leading us on this journey and will mold and form this process to you and your needs.

My Own Process

In my own times of waiting on God sometimes I will worship for fifteen or twenty minutes first. Other times I may pray in tongues for an hour or so. Sometimes I will pray much longer. We have to always follow the voice of the spirit in this process.

When I move to the next phase of waiting on God, I go sit in my prayer chair. I will be honest and tell you that I have heard from many who see in the spiritual realm that almost all of them had prayer chairs so I decided it must be important. It is. When I sit in my chair I take a minute to relax and get as comfortable as possible .The reasoning here is when we wait on God we are trying to focus on Him and His Kingdom. If we are kneeling, after a while it can hurt or feel uncomfortable and that shifts the focus from God to our discomfort. If we are lifting our hands, eventually our arms may get tired and again our focus is shifted from the spiritual to the physical. We are making it as easy as we can to stay our minds and hearts on Him.

We remain motionless. Why? Once again, if we are shifting positions, scratching ourselves or stretching etc., it takes our minds and focus back to the physical realm. Like anything you try to learn it's important to stay focused. The Bible says that a double minded man is unstable. We won't make the connection to the spiritual if our focus is all over the map. Ok...So we are still. How still?

Physically Still

Physically you should be so still that it might be a bit difficult to stay awake at first. Purposely relax. Check yourself out and see if there is any muscle that is tight or any part that needs to relax. Relax. Now as you remain still, <u>you should not be moving at all</u> . I don't mean don't move very much, I mean don't move period. What you are trying to do is leave the physical behind so to speak and embrace the spirit. If you remain still for very long you will begin to feel your spirit man. We normally live in the physical but when we're still we can engage the spiritual.

Sometimes when you are this still, it *is* difficult to stay awake. You may fall asleep many times as you practice this waiting on the Lord. That's o.k. As you continue you will become adjusted to the feeling and you'll remain awake and alert.

Quiet Your Mind

This sounds kind of strange to some but there is really nothing strange about it. You are not emptying your mind, you are just not thinking about or dwelling on things that are not related or helpful to this exercise. We put the things of the day aside. We focus on the Lord and if our mind, thoughts or imagination gets off track we bring our thoughts back into line. This can be a real process for us.

In everyday life most of us are constantly surrounded by noise and movement and it is sometimes difficult at first to adjust to the stillness and quiet. But it gets much easier with practice. And frankly, as you begin to see into the spiritual realm the "effort" of being still doesn't seem like as much of a sacrifice any more.

The scripture says…

Casting down imaginations, and every high thing that exalteth itself against the knowledge of God, and bringing into captivity every thought to the obedience of Christ (2 Corinthians 10:5)

The more that your time and your senses and spirit are filled with the things of God, the easier it is to accomplish this. It's when we look at things that are not helpful or convenient that those things try to invade our prayer time and derail us from getting closer to the Lord and the things of the Lord.

Stillness

I cannot overemphasize this aspect of waiting. When we are still in our body…physically still and still in our soul…i.e. our thoughts, desires and emotions etc., it allows our spirit man to engage without opposition. It is a process normally for most (it was for me also) but this is very attainable.

It can be easy to fall asleep when you are this still. Basically for all practical purposes your body is asleep but your spirit and mind are not. I may have a chair that I use to wait but others lay down on their bed or on the floor. I also lay on the floor to wait on God as it is easier for me to stay awake if I am not in my bed. Experiment and *enjoy* this process. I promise you that the Lord won't let you down!

Draw nigh to God, and he will draw nigh to you. Cleanse your hands, ye sinners; and purify your hearts, ye double minded. (James 4:8)

If You Fall Asleep

Here is a **powerful key** that I learned late in my education in spiritual sight. If you are in the process of waiting on God and you suddenly wake up and realize that you fell asleep. Don't call it quits! Start again! And if you fall asleep again, when you awake you begin again. Do this as much as you are able. What eventually happens is that your body becomes too tired to wake up but your spirit is still desiring to engage or to see, so your spirit man will "wake up" and your spiritual eyes will open.

When this happens try to remain calm. (again, there is an adjustment) As you remain calm, the experience will continue and you will grow in it. If you get too excited your soul will pull you back.

3

CULTIVATING AWARENESS

Awareness is another thing that you must train yourself in. You might think that if you saw something in the spirit such as an angel, that you could not miss it. The truth is we miss it every day because we don't really know what we should be looking for.

Many times we go through our day seeing things and immediately dismissing them without a second thought about it. A flash of light...something that we might see out of the corner of our eye... a color that "seems" to surround someone. These are all the beginnings of seeing into the spiritual realm. The problem is that we have no experience and very little teaching about this subject and we do dismiss virtually every spiritual thing that we see .

Our Eyes Playing Tricks On Us

Most of us have been trained from the time we were young to dismiss the spiritual things that we saw. We have been told "It's not real" or "It's just your imagination" so many times that that becomes our mind-set. We must break that mind-set off of us and create a new one that embraces and celebrates the spiritual realm and is **aware** of it.

A Prayer

Father, I'm sorry for dismissing spiritual things that I see. Father let every ungodly mind-set about the spiritual world be broken off of my life. Let every scale and veil that was formed by this unbelief be removed from my eyes. Father give me an enhanced awareness of the spiritual realm and the things of the spirit. Father give me "eyes to see" according to your word. Teach me to be more aware every day and give me grace to walk in this reality. Let your angels manifest their presence openly in my life and let every obstruction of the enemy be removed. In Jesus' name, Amen.

Practical Applications

There are several things that I have learned to do on an ongoing basis that allows me to be aware and to see the angels around my life as well as to see the enemy. Things that I seemingly stumbled upon but in reality it was the Holy Spirit teaching me.

First Glances

When you first wake up in the morning, continue to lay in bed and be still. Be just as still as if you were still asleep. Slowly look around the room and examine the atmosphere. Look for any disturbance in the atmosphere. A subtle shift of some kind or a slight variation of color for example.

For me as well as others, the spirit realm looks very similar to heat rising off of a black top roa

d on a hot summer day. There is a "buckling" of the air so to speak. Look for things like that. As you begin to see these things (and you will) if you examine them in a relaxed but attentive manner, they will begin to expand in color or clarity. The forms will be more apparent and solid. What starts out looking like absolutely nothing can be revealed to be something quite spectacular.

A Testimony

One morning in mid- June 2015, I woke up and did exactly what I'm asking you to do. I laid still and slowly opened my eyes. The atmosphere was dawn, which is an even better backdrop for seeing bright spiritual things. I noticed that the atmosphere to the side of my bed looked just a little strange so I focused on that area and kept watching. After a few minutes, my spiritual vision became much clearer and I could now see that two angelic figures were standing in the room not far from our bed. It at first appeared that they might have been talking to each other, but when they saw that I was looking at them, they turned their attention to me. The angel on the right shifted his position and watched to see if my eyes followed him. When he saw that they did, he flew away. The second angel did the same thing. Had I not taken the time to be aware of the spiritual atmosphere in the room when I first woke up I would not have seen them at all. I might have even seen the air in the room shift but would have dismissed it as my eyes playing tricks on me.

Why did the angels look to see if I could see them and why did they leave? I have an idea about it. You see angels are not all-knowing like God. They don't always know if you see them right away. This is especially true if you are still in the process of exercising your spiritual senses and just breaking through so to speak. Many times angels will be very close to your face when your spiritual eyes open, looking into your eyes. This has happened to me and I'm sure it will happen to you.

The reason I think they "leave" or make it so you can't see them is because it probably does not serve a purpose for God for you to see them at that point. I opened my eyes once to see the angel standing guard over us and just as soon as he saw me looking at him, he stepped through the wall to where I couldn't see him. I thought about it and decided that he probably did that so I would go back to sleep and get some rest. I'm know for a fact that I would have stayed up all night gawking at him had he not done so. These are all things we adjust to day by day.

Coming and Going

Because virtually all of our interaction throughout the course of the day is in the physical realm we rarely think about seeing the spiritual. As we go to work or the store or any other places we must begin to cultivate a habit of looking at the spiritual realm in these places. You should purposely look for the spiritual atmosphere in every building you walk into. Examine every room you enter and every gathering you attend. (especially church or gatherings of believers)

Although it is difficult and I'm not saying that you should do this, I will look at the spiritual atmosphere in my peripheral vision when I am traveling in a car. You don't divert your attention from the road or your driving duties but rather just keep an awareness about you concerning that realm. What my wife and I have noticed lately (August 2015) is columns of light going from the earth into the clouds. Some of them have been quite large and they are obviously a spiritual manifestation.

The atmosphere around your house is a great place to practice being aware. While doing your yardwork or even sitting out on your patio for/at the spiritual realm you can see some pretty amazing things.

Because you make a conscious effort to do this I believe that the Lord helps you. We are told to seek those things that are above. The Lord isn't blocking us from this, He is helping us.

If ye then be risen with Christ, seek those things which are above, where Christ sitteth on the right hand of God. (Colossians 3:1)

Evening and Night

As your day winds down and you begin to relax, read a book or watch a television program, these are times when we are more still than normal and we can see better than if we are doing some other more vigorous activities. I have seen both the angelic and the demonic while watching TV.

Take a minute every so often and look around the room. Cultivate an awareness of the spiritual real through constant purposeful engagement.

At night or dusk, the light level makes it harder to focus on the natural things around us. If the room is dark, you can't see the natural very well. That's why it's a perfect time to look for the spiritual. If you take a little time every night in prayer, open your eyes and look around every so often.

As you do these things on a constant basis you are training yourself to acknowledge this realm This small step will bring greater clarity of spiritual sight From morning 'til night and in the middle of the night always be aware of the atmosphere around you.

This awareness can easily be applied to all of your spiritual senses. You might start with sight and as it begins to increase you could also pay attention to sounds or smells, tastes or feelings.

4

ESTABLISHING THE ATMOSPHERE

If you are desiring to see, make sure to give yourself a wonderful atmosphere to look at when your spiritual eyes are opened. The places where you spend the most time such as home or work, are areas that you can establish a heavenly atmosphere. This is done in several different ways and you may have your own ideas as well. Every legal right that you have as a child of God should be used to set the environment around you and your family.

For our purposes I will say home but it could be anywhere. The fact is that everywhere the sole of your foot treads is given to you as a child of God. You can exercise your authority to change things.

The Blood

Start by applying (or declaring) the blood of Jesus over your home and property. Apply the blood over every room, every hallway, every space and closet. Go into these rooms when you do it. You are making a strong statement in the spiritual realm when you do. Anything that the Holy Spirit brings to mind as you do this, apply the blood of Jesus over it. (this includes people of course)

Anointing

This can be done at the same time that you apply the blood of Jesus. Release the anointing of the Holy Spirit into your home and into each room or place that you pray over.

Anointing Oil

Anoint your home with oil. Anoint every doorway, every room, every chair and everything that you feel led to anoint. I also walk the boundaries of my property and anoint that as well. Members of the house should be anointed as well as your animals.

Continuous Praise

In our home we play anointed worship and praise music as much as we can. For about a two year period we played worship music twenty-four hours a day, seven days a week. This almost sounds impossible especially if not everyone is onboard so to speak. Here is what I did and what I recommend as you try to put this into practice.

First of all realize that it does no good to play worship music that does not establish the right atmosphere. If people are upset because they are trying to have a conversation and can't hear due to the worship music, that isn't what you want. Play the music at a normal level if you are actually singing along or worshipping. If no one is going to be home you can turn up the volume and let the angels enjoy it. The rest of the time, play the music so soft that if someone came into your home they might say *"You know it almost sounds like there's music playing ..."*

If you play the music very softly, it still makes a difference in the spiritual realm and that's the important thing.

We had an assortment of anointed worship CDs that we put on continuous play all throughout the house on four different CD players. Use what the Holy Spirit reveals to you. We used Benny Hinn, Joann McFatter, Kimberly and Alberto Riviera, Bethel worship, Hillsong music and others too.

Sound the Shofar

My wife really felt like she was supposed to have a shofar so we got one. I was not immediately aware of how powerful the sound of the shofar is but we soon learned. The very first night that we sounded the shofar, my son saw three huge balls of light "fall" into our neighborhood just minutes later. The second time, I saw many angels gather in my prayer room. After I realized that the angels were responding to the sound of the shofar, I began to sound it a lot more. We sound the shofar all throughout our home on a regular basis. It makes a **tangible** difference in the atmosphere. If you do this you will notice it too.

Prayer, Decrees and Declarations

And of course we must saturate ourselves and our homes and families with prayer. Pray without and pray blessings over your home. Decree the atmosphere of Heaven. Release the government of the Kingdom of Heaven in your home and environment. Make declarative statements about your home and family. <u>The best way to do this is to use the scriptures because they are very powerful.</u>

And if it seem evil unto you to serve the LORD, choose you this day whom ye will serve; whether the gods which your fathers served that were on the other side of the flood, or the gods of the Amorites, in whose land ye dwell: **but as for me and my house, we will serve the LORD.** *(Joshua 24:15)*

And all thy children shall be taught of the LORD; and **great shall be the peace of thy children**. *(Isaiah 54:13)*

I know thy works: behold, **I have set before thee an open door, and no man can shut it:** *for thou hast a little strength, and hast kept my word, and hast not denied my name. (Revelation 3:8)*

5

IMAGINATION

Imagination is another powerful key in the quest for spiritual sight. Many people think that using the imagination is just pretending to see something but anyone who understands something about the spiritual realm will tell you that the imagination is a door or access point.

We have often heard "It's just your imagination" as a dismissive phrase on par with unimportant or unreal. The imagination, sanctified by God is a wonderful thing. The Bible tells us to

Casting down imaginations, and every high thing that exalteth itself against the knowledge of God, *and bringing into captivity every thought to the obedience of Christ; (2 Corinthians 10:5)*

The Bible doesn't tell us to cast down imaginations but rather those that exalt themselves against the knowledge of God.

Sanctification

The imagination must be sanctified. Anyone who has ever seen a television show has more than likely seen things that defile the imagination and our eyes. If you see garbage your spiritual eyes can become damaged. That's why the Lord tells us to look at those things unseen and to think about holy and pure things.

*Finally, brethren, whatsoever things are true, whatsoever things are honest, whatsoever things are just, whatsoever things are pure, whatsoever things are lovely, whatsoever things are of good report; if there be any virtue, and if there be any praise, **think on these things.** Philippians 4:8)*

A Prayer

Father, Please forgive me for anything that my eyes have seen that defiled me or offended you. Please forgive me for using my imagination for wrong purposes and make it clean now by the blood of Jesus. Cleanse me and heal me now and I thank you for it in Jesus' name. Amen.

Using the Imagination

Using the imagination is a very simple process and we don't do it any differently when using it for God.

If I asked you to remember what your house looks like and describe it to me, you might close your eyes and try to "see" it in your mind. This is how we use the imagination. We see a mental picture or imagine something. In using the imagination for Godly purposes we can do it many different ways. I will give you some and I really suggest that you try all of them.

Going into the Word

To practice seeing with the spiritual eyes or the eyes of our imagination we can do so by observing Bible scenes first hand. Take a favorite scripture and meditate on it. Perhaps you would like to visit the encounter that the Lord had with the disciples when he cooked fish for them after He has risen. (John Ch. 21)

In your mind you might see the Lord making the fire and the boat out on the water. You could even smell the food cooking. Read the entire passage several times and each time close your eyes and try to see it a little clearer with a little more detail. Like anything it gets easier with practice.

It Sure *Feels* Pretend

It may feel like you are doing nothing but pretending and wasting your time. What you have to remember is that Jesus said the imagination was reality. When Jesus talked about lusting in your heart in Matthew chapter five, He said you have already committed adultery. He didn't say you have thought about or imagined committing adultery. The fact that if you do something in your imagination it is reality may be scary for some. *"Do you mean I have to keep my thoughts pure and clean 24/7?* Yes. Yes you do. The scriptures tell us that as you already know. (Philippians 4:8)

Also, keep in mind that I'm not just sharing a bunch of good ideas that I have heard. Everything I teach has been my revelation from God. The Lord personally taught me about sight in this way as I share it with you. Everything that the Lord has told me works. Imagine that!

So please set aside any doubt or unbelief about using your imagination. This is just part of adjusting to walking in the spiritual realm. Generally the only time we have purposefully engaged the spiritual realm has been when we have worshipped or prayed and even then most of us were never really aware of the real significance at the time.

Make it Real

When you use your imagination, two very important things to keep in mind are... 1. Make it as real as possible even if it requires a little work to get to that place. It won't drop into your lap unless you just have a gift for dreaming. And 2... try to make your images match up with your prayers. Don't pray one thing and think another. Keep your focus all going in the same direction.

To do this is a discipline and usually takes practice.

It's not that you are striving to earn anything from God but rather you are positioning yourself to better receive and see it come to pass.

Imagination for Healing

Any time that you lift someone up in prayer, also use your imagination. Imagine yourself laying hands on them and the power of God flowing into their bodies. Feel the virtue leaving you as you pray. See the countenance change as they are healed. See angels coming to minister to them.

Imagination for Prayer in General

Regardless of what you are praying about always get your imagination onboard with your prayer. God sees your thoughts. He knows you. Let your passion for the situation be manifested as you pray.

Imagination Prayer Walks

I learned this a couple of years after the Lord first really began to open my eyes. When I would pray at night over my family, I would walk around the house as I prayed. I would pray over every room and everyone. I did this over and over, night after night. One night I did this and when I came back to my starting position at my prayer chair I saw that my body had never gotten up to pray. My spirit had gotten up to pray and my spirit man had walked through the house for thirty minutes or so praying over the whole house.

After I realized that my spirit was that desirous to pray, I began to purposely position myself for my spirit man to pray through the house. I would sit in my prayer chair and imagine walking through the house praying. The more I did this, the more that it began to happen.

I will tell you though that it was an adjustment for me. The first time this happened I was fearful that this was a permanent situation and spent a good five minutes shaking myself with all of my might to wake up my physical body. Now that I know what's going on a little better I know that **being at peace and trusting God is the way we should handle things or act in every circumstance.**

Imagine The Lord and His Angels

In opening our spiritual eyes and in using the imagination another great key is to imagine conversing with the Lord. Ask Him questions. Minister to the Lord Worship Him. Tell Him your desires and goals and truly cultivate a bond. Also, imagine the angels that are around your life. When you go to bed imagine the angels that stand guard over you and what they look like. What expression is on their faces? How many are there? What are their names? Ask them and find out! The thing to remember is we are trying to make the spiritual realm as normal for us as possible and make walking in the spirit as normal as possible. This process of using imagination is a powerful way to do that. So do it purposely and continually!

6

PRAYER AND FASTING

If there was ever a vehicle that will take you where you need to go, it's prayer. We have a history of the miraculous through speaking to God in prayer. Prayer does change things. In the book of Isaiah it talks about Hezekiah turning his face to the wall. This is talking about getting serious in prayer. God heard him and answered. I used the example of Hezekiah because we need to have that kind of passion and commitment when we pray. If you pray with your entire being you will see things you have never seen before.

If we are going to pray we might as well give it all we have. If we don't have that level of passion, we should ask the Lord to give it to us. In pursuing spiritual sight or greater spiritual sight we have to have the passion for it. If there is any part of you that is blasé about this don't expect spectacular results.

So our prayers should be fueled by passion and proof of passion is time spent in pursuit. Just like in anything we desire, the time spent will make a difference in success or failure.

Focused Prayer

Many times we don't see breakthrough in something because we are following a pattern we learned in church or in our homes about how to pray instead of from the word of God. Examine most prayer and they are very short in they are focused and still short if they are not focused.

Even at prayer meetings I have seldom heard someone pray longer than five minutes. At church, opening or closing the service or praying over an offering is rarely if ever over five minutes. This becomes our model much of the time because people we consider very Godly are praying these short prayers and we get our ideas from them much of the time.

Jesus had a ministry that was unsurpassed yet He said "Greater things, you will do..." Jesus spent incredible amounts of time in the secret place, alone with the Father. Even the start of His ministry was **40 days of prayer and fasting**. We need to learn to bring our prayer life to that level if we want to see.

This is sometimes a very unpopular message but **we have to sacrifice our time** if we are to see clearly in the spiritual realm.

I had some experiences where the fire of God had fallen on me and after having seen it and experienced it, I had a strong desire for it again...and again. One night I sat in my prayer chair for a couple of hours just praying "Lord sanctify me" over and over. After about two hours of this **very focused prayer**, my spiritual eyes opened and I saw the spiritual veils in front of me. I watched in fascination as the closest veil disintegrated and fell to the ground.

This was one of the many telling experiences that allowed me to see that focused prayer for an extended period of time yields great fruit.

Fasting

Fasting is a denial of the physical and soulish life so that the spirit man is unhindered as we seek spiritual things. I believe that because of the days we are living in you will very probably need to fast for certain breakthroughs. The enemy does not want you to see in the spiritual realm and he will oppose you. Fasting is a way to gain spiritual strength and overcome.

As you deny the wants of the body and soul by fasting, we must also feed the spirit man for strengthening. Worship, prayer, Bible study and meditation on the Word of God are all great things to strengthen our spirits.

To be very honest, there are few things that will open your spiritual eyes faster than prayer combined with fasting.

The fasting could be a meal, a day, a week or longer. Fasting from solid food is good. You could drink water only, or if you need to for health or strength reasons you could have liquids in some form such as fruit or vegetable juices or broths. Be led of the Spirit.

The prayer part of this combination should be a different kind of prayer. Pray a prayer of faith. Use this time to decree as you pray that you do see the unseen, you do interact with angels and you do visit heavenly places. Declare the scriptures that are promises to us as you pray. I have found this to be very effective also. The week that I began declaring "I see angels all the time" I had a marked increase in the angelic activity that I did see. So **speak these things out in faith** according to the word.

*And Jesus answered them, "Have faith in God. Truly, I say to you, whoever says to this mountain, 'Be taken up and thrown into the sea,' and does not doubt in his heart, **but believes that what he says will come to pass,** it will be done for him. Therefore I tell you, whatever you ask in prayer, **<u>believe that you have received it,</u> and it will be yours.** (Mark 11:22-24)*

Times of prayer and fasting should be accompanied by Bible study and worship and waiting on God.

Going Overboard

I would be remiss if I didn't at least reveal this to you and let you make up your own mind about it. In the days of the early church and even now I would guess, monks and other orders who were devoted to prayer would often tie themselves in an upright position so that they could pray all night without falling asleep.

The times that I have prayed through the night have been times of great breakthrough for me. **There is something about denying our body sleep that lowers the spiritual veils** and allows for greater access to the spiritual realm. My son had several days at work where they needed him to work around the clock and after two days with hardly any sleep, he said he could openly see the spiritual realm.

One important thing to keep in mind is that you should not abstain from sleep if you have other responsibilities such as driving or doing anything that requires physical alertness.

If you have a weekend that you can press into God, then would be the perfect time to fast, pray and "watch" through the night. The combination of the three is very powerful to open your spiritual eyes.

Just Do What You Can

Do not feel disqualified in any way if you cannot do the things I suggest exactly as I suggest them. Just do what you are able to do and God will honor that.

He is training us and He knows what we are capable of and what the true desires of our hearts are.

In times of prayer and fasting and watching through the night, your eyes will be opened and you will engage the spiritual realm in a way that is **faith filled and real.** That is, the reality of the spirit realm is so overwhelming that it makes the physical realm seem dull.

When this happens our faith rises to a level beyond what we are used to experiencing and we see prayers answered and we (by the spirit) know what we should pray.

From this place of connection, I have seen God answer many prayers with miraculous results.

7

JOURNALING YOUR EXPERIENCES

There is hardly a better way to show yourself and the Lord that you value what he is doing in your life than journaling. The Bible says...

And the LORD answered me: "Write the vision; make it plain on tablets, so he may run who reads it. (Habakkuk 2:2)

Journaling what God is doing will encourage you to press in for more. You will "run" when you read it. Many times we can have the most extraordinary experiences and forget all about them. Even if you are able to have a vague recollection, it's not the same as a full recounting with all the details. There is power in a testimony. When you re-read your testimonies it makes room for similar things.

Personal Experience

I had a couple of days where I began to feel sorry for myself. I felt that I was going through a dry time and I didn't like it. The problem was, I was wrong. I went into my journal to encourage myself and after reading it I "remembered" that I had had a wonderful visitation from angel only less than two weeks earlier! I had forgotten it! That is another reason to journal.

Increase Will Come

The thing that I have found that is most encouraging is that our awareness increases the more we journal about our experiences. You have to be thorough as you go. Write down every little supernatural thing that happens in your life. Don't say "Well, that was only a little flash of light" or "The orb was only visible for a few seconds" and then not record it. No, you must record everything. As you do this it will begin to increase in greater measure and frequency.

If you hardly see at all, you may be writing down things like " I felt a cool breeze while praying" or " I saw a brief flash of light across the room". As you faithfully honor these events enough to record them you will soon be writing things like "I saw a part of an angel" or I saw an angel today" The honor you show to the event says that you have value for it. If it means something to you it will find a place in your life and enlarge. You can count on it.

A Step of Faith

Recently I spoke with a man that told me that these things did not work for him and he could not see. I began asking questions to see what went wrong. After asking several questions, I asked him what the last entry in his journal was. He responded *"Why would I even buy a journal if nothing is happening?"*

This walk in the supernatural things of God is definitely a walk of faith. When we buy the journal we are making a statement. We are saying *"I believe that God is going to do things in my life that are important enough that I need to write them down."* When we lay the journal and pen out by our bed or table we are saying that we are ready for what God is going to do.

You see the man that said it didn't work didn't actually do it. He had made up his mind not to buy the journal until *after* things began to happen. That is not a step of faith!

What You Should Write

As you journal, record your experiences but also record your prayer times. Record your times of worship and praise. Record the date and time and the duration of the time spent waiting on God or in prayer. This way, you have a way to determine what Is working for you. You can see what the fruit is as you go. Record your failures as well as your successes because that will show you what not to do.

In my own journals I have documented that the more time I spend in prayer and waiting on God the more visitations I have and supernatural experiences. On the negative side, I have found that if I have days that are filled with problems of the world my prayer times are not as fruitful. I believe because my attention is divided.

My Own Journal Entries.

I generally record my experiences in spiral notebooks now because using the nice leather bound journals began to get too expensive. I have probably thirty notebooks and journals all together. Since I began this journey my entries in my journal cover everything from sparkles hanging in mid-air to heavenly gemstones to visitations from angels and the Lord himself. We have seen orbs of light in all colors and sizes, lightening shooting through our house and angels appearing as men. Sometimes even while writing these accounts or writing for my books I have had gold appear on my hand or desk.

The point is that I believe that you can have all of these things and more. God is no respecter of persons. (Acts 10:34) What He does for me He will do for you. I truly believe that if you will take these simple but powerful keys and really use them that spiritual sight and the supernatural realm will open to you. Many have this idea that if God wanted me to see He would just make me see. That is rarely the case. If God wanted you to see He would have given you eyes, which He did! We just need to learn!

8

PUTTING IT ALL TOGETHER

Having given you these keys I would be remiss if I didn't give you a little more information on how best to use them and put them all together. I know with just having this rather basic knowledge that it's still going to require a lot of trial and error and figuring out what works best for you.

These are all things that I have had to learn as I went and the Lord did teach me these things but I had to "come into them" so to speak through practice and engagement.

Many times early on I would hear someone talk about spiritual sight and the instruction was just unclear enough to be frustrating. We don't want that.

An Overview

As you start your day, start it by opening your eyes and looking for or at the spiritual realm. Do this for at least five minutes every morning without fail. We will be training ourselves to walk in both realms at all times.

As you get ready for your day, Pray! Apply the blood of Jesus. Pray over your life in every way that you can. Pray in tongues. You can pray as you get ready. I always do this and then pray or praise on the way to work every day. As you start your day, make sure to look around you at least several times an hour and try to see if you can see the spiritual realm or the angels around you. When you leave your house, make sure that your praise or worship music is playing. Let the angels be happy that they were assigned to you. Give them a nice place to be through worship and praise.

When you get to work or wherever you happen to go, apply the blood of Jesus over the place and release the government and the atmosphere of Heaven upon the place. By doing this you are making the atmosphere thick with the things of Heaven. We are making it easier to see the Heavenly things because we are filling the atmosphere with Heaven. We overwhelm the atmosphere so that we can't help but see something.

As you go through your workday, remember who you are and release the love of God in your workplace. Look for the angels there. Every time you walk into a different room be aware of the spiritual atmosphere.

If you are able, take a break during the course of the day and lift your hands in worship. Angels love to be around those who worship God. Even if you have to go into a bathroom stall to do it, do it!

As you drive home, ask God to highlight to you who the redeemed are in the cars around you. Look for small to medium sized orbs of light just above the drivers of the cars. (I have seen this while driving) Ask God to show you signs in the Heavens as you go.

When you get home, again survey the spiritual climate in and around your home. Look and study the atmosphere at least for a bit to train yourself and to stay engaged.

If you have a shofar, blow it several times all the while realizing that your spirit is sending out a message through the sound. The breath of God (the Holy Spirit) is sounding through the ram's horn.

After you have finished make an announcement to the angels who show (whether you can see them or not) and tell them "Angels I just wanted you to know we appreciate your involvement in our lives and we welcome you into our home to do the will of God. Please feel free to come any time.

Make sure the praise music is still playing even if

you have to lower the volume.

Remember to **pray without ceasing**. If your tongue is not otherwise engaged, keep praying in tongues. Sometimes six, eight or ten hours a day is possible without even having to set aside time. For those of you who drive a lot, you can continually pray while you drive.

All the while, as you spend time with your family, **realize** that the Lord is with you. He never leaves you and be consciously aware of that. Also **be aware** that angels are always around as you enjoy your evening, at home or wherever you go.

Make sure and read the word even if only a chapter to keep feeding your spirit. As you go to sleep, think about the word and ask God for greater revelation of that word. Ask for the things you desire. The Bible says we have not because we ask not (James 4:2) Ask for clear sight and to hear God's voice. Ask for Heavenly encounters and visitations of angels. Ask for all the plans and blessings of God for your life to be manifested.

When you lay down to sleep, frame a picture in your mind of Heaven. Tell the Lord you want to see it.

Get up during the night watch, two, three or four o'clock and pray and wait on God for an hour or two. Sit in stillness and look for God to show you something. This is always a very productive time for those who see into the Heavenly realms. Make this a practice and commit to at least a couple days a week.

A Bit Extreme

I hope that after reading the overview that you are **not** thinking it to be extreme. Throughout this short book of instruction, we are trying to establish a constant awareness and involvement with the spiritual realm. If I were to tell you that as you go about your day make sure to keep your physical eyes open, you might think "Of course! How would I see if I walked around with them closed!"

That's the point. Spiritual sight is not an occasional dip into the things of God but a constant state of being. You are being a child of God who lives from a position in Christ where He has provided **all** things pertaining to life and Godliness.

According as his divine power hath given unto us all things that pertain unto life and godliness, through the knowledge of him that hath called us to glory and virtue: (2 Peter 1:3)

In my own life I practice what I have preached here. It works. The more time you spend drawing nigh to Him the closer He draws to you.

I pray that you are blessed beyond anything you could ask or dream!

A Prayer

Father, I pray that you would empower each and every person who reads this book or this prayer with power from on high. Remove the veils and the scales from their eyes and give them clear spiritual vision. Apply the eye salve of Revelation 3:18 to the eyes of the reader and give them grace to walk in this reality for the glory of God. Let their eyes be cleansed, sanctified and consecrated for your purpose and plans and bless them beyond measure.

In Jesus' name. Amen

About The Author

Michael Van Vlymen is an author and speaker who has a deep passion to share that everyone can experience the supernatural things of God. Michael is the author of "Angelic Visitations and Supernatural Encounters", "How to do Spiritual Warfare" and "How to See in the Spirit" a best-seller on the subject of spiritual sight.

Other Books by This Author

How to See in the Spirit

How to do Spiritual Warfare

Angelic Visitations and Supernatural Encounters

Soraya Limon
(708) 668-8250

Made in the USA
Lexington, KY
12 July 2011